LIFETIMES: UNDER APARTHEID

LIFETIMES
UNDER APARTHEID

NADINE GORDIMER
DAVID GOLDBLATT

ALFRED A. KNOPF
New York 1986

THIS IS A BORZOI BOOK
PUBLISHED BY ALFRED A. KNOPF, INC.

Grateful acknowledgment is made to the following for permission to reprint previously published material:
From *Burger's Daughter* by Nadine Gordimer. Copyright © 1979 by Nadine Gordimer. Reprinted by permission of Viking Penguin, Inc. From *The Conservationist* by Nadine Gordimer. Copyright © 1962, 1963 by Nadine Gordimer. Reprinted by permission of Viking Penguin, Inc. From *July's People* by Nadine Gordimer. Copyright © 1981 by Nadine Gordimer. Reprinted by permission of Viking Penguin, Inc. From *The Late Bourgeois World* by Nadine Gordimer. Copyright © 1966 by Nadine Gordimer. Reprinted by permission of Viking Penguin, Inc. Selections from "Good Climate, Friendly Inhabitants," "The Last Kiss," "The Life of the Imagination," "Something for the Time Being," "Which New Era Would That Be," and "Ah, Woe Is Me" are from *Selected Stories* by Nadine Gordimer. Copyright 1952, © 1956, 1957, 1959, 1960, 1961, 1964, 1965, 1968, 1969, 1971, 1975 by Nadine Gordimer. Reprinted by permission of Viking Penguin, Inc. From "Monday Is Better Than Sunday" in *The Soft Voice of the Serpent* by Nadine Gordimer. Copyright 1950, 1951, 1952 by Nadine Gordimer. Reprinted by permission of Viking Penguin, Inc. From "Oral History" in *A Soldier's Embrace* by Nadine Gordimer. This selection originally appeared in *Playboy* magazine. Copyright © 1977 by Nadine Gordimer. Reprinted by permission of Viking Penguin, Inc. From "A Soldier's Embrace" in *A Soldier's Embrace* by Nadine Gordimer. This selection originally appeared in *Harper's* magazine. Copyright © 1976 by Nadine Gordimer. Reprinted by permission of Viking Penguin, Inc. From *Occasion for Loving* by Nadine Gordimer. Copyright © 1960, 1963 by Nadine Gordimer. Reprinted by permission of Viking Penguin, Inc. From *Something Out There* by Nadine Gordimer. Copyright © 1979, 1981, 1982, 1983, 1984 by Nadine Gordimer. Reprinted by permission of Viking Penguin, Inc.

Library of Congress Cataloging-in-Publication Data

Gordimer, Nadine.
Lifetimes: under apartheid.

1. Gordimer, Nadine—Quotations. 2. Apartheid—
South Africa—Fiction. 3. Apartheid—South Africa—
Pictorial works. 4. South Africa—Description and
travel—1966- —Views. I. Goldblatt, David.
II. Title.
PR9369.3.G6A6   823   86-45303
ISBN 0-394-55406-X

Manufactured in Germany

FIRST EDITION

Printed in West Germany by Universitätsdruckerei H. Stürtz AG

We should like to record our grateful thanks to Frank Platt, whose idea this book was, and whose indefatigable enthusiasm and efforts have achieved it. Richard Benson and Thomas Palmer have been unstinting in the time and interest they have devoted to the project, Benson in the care and art with which he has made the negatives for the reproduction of the photographs, Palmer for his dedicated concern for the layout and printing of this book. We wish to record our deepest gratitude.

Nadine Gordimer
David Goldblatt

There our house was; and I lived in it as I lived in my body.

The Lying Days, 1953

At 1510A Emdeni South, Soweto, August 1972.

We have come a long way, with our country: a lifetime. Both of us were born white and slowly learned to leave that fatal isolation through the lessons of our work: the images and words.

We believe that what white South Africans have done to black South Africans seeps like an indelible stain through fiction and photographs. The repression and tragedy of black lives is there; we did not have to look for it, only to let it reveal itself as honestly and deeply as we could. The distortion and coarsening that white people brought upon themselves is there. These cannot be hidden; the image and word give back what is behind the face and place. For us, the images and words in this book move with what they depict, to an end that was always present. It is just not possible to live *that way*. Now the country is on the edge of an unspeakably cruel civil war. It is also on the threshold of the new life that must come; the disaster is that the war need never, should never, have been.

Nadine Gordimer
David Goldblatt

Ever since I had begun to see the natives all around not as furniture, trees, or the casual landmarks of a road through which my life was passing, but as faces; the faces of old men, of girls, of children; ever since they had stepped up all around me, as they do, silently, at some point in the life of every white person who lives in South Africa, something had been working in me. The slow corrosive guilt, a guilt personal and inherited, amorphous as the air and particular as the tone of your own voice, which, admitted or denied, is in all white South Africans. The Nationalist farmers who kicked and beat their convict African labourers had it and it was in me. Like an obscure pain we can't confess we clutch to it this counter-irritant, or that. One pretence is kinder than another, that is all. With kicks and curses you may keep the guilt at a distance, with a show of the tenderness of my own skin, I may clasp it like a hair shirt.

The Lying Days, 1953

The road on which I had hesitated before going down to the Concession Stores that Saturday afternoon was the road between Mine and town. I passed along it going to school every morning. I came back along it at two o'clock every afternoon in the bus which had shaken past first the Town Hall in its geometrical setting of flower beds and frostbitten lawn and municipal coat-of-arms grown in tight fleshy cactus; the dirty shopblinds of the main street making a chalky dazzle; the native delivery boys sitting in the gutters, staring at their broken shoes; the buildings, like a familiar tune picked out silently on a keyboard: one, one, two-storey, two, one, one-storey — then the houses of the township, long rows of corrugated iron roofs behind bullet-headed municipal trees shorn regularly to keep them free of the telephone wires, the Greek shop with its pyramid of crude pink coconut buns and frieze of spotted bananas, the doctor's house with a tiled roof and a tennis court; and out at last, past the last row of houses turning their backyards — a patchwork of washing, a broken dog kennel, the little one-eyed room where the servant lived — to the veld.

The Lying Days, 1953

Somewhere away from the houses resting back round the square of the Recreation Hall, beyond the pines in the road and the gums sounding, over the dry veld and in the town, Olwen was putting on a blue crinoline hat. Who could believe it was happening the same time as the doves spread their fat breasts in comfortable dust baths in the garden? Everything was waiting for me to answer. "Helen! You must make up your mind what you want to do. You know I can't leave you on your own, the girl's out." Yes, I knew that, an unwritten law so sternly upheld and generally accepted that it would occur to no child to ask why: a little girl must not be left alone because there were native boys about. That was all. Native boys were harmless and familiar because they were servants, or delivery boys bringing the groceries or the fish by bicycle from town, or Mine boys something to laugh at in their blankets and their clay-spiked hair, but at the same time they spoke and shouted in a language you didn't understand and dressed differently in any old thing, and so were mysterious. Not being left alone because they were about was simply something to do with their mysteriousness.

The Lying Days, 1953

The road back is commonplace and familiar enough to bring anyone down to earth. The white working man knows he couldn't live as well anywhere else in the world, and the blacks want shoes on their feet — where else in Africa will you see so many well-shod blacks as on this road? There is a bus-stop for them (beer cartons strewn) and here, ten yards on, a bus-stop for whites employed round about: just as counting sheep puts you to sleep so ticking off a familiar progression of objects can be used to restore concentration. A prefabricated shelter at the whites' bus-stop and from the background of a well-known cigarette advertisement someone stands forward and — again — he has that peculiar inescapable sense that eyes are fixed on him as target or goal. No. A girl's face; a young woman is standing there, and the eyes claim him and, nearer (he has slowed automatically, out of distraction rather than curiosity) he can see clearly that although she is not actually smiling the corners of her rather big mouth are curled in a suppressed greeting. No no. He's not quick enough to accelerate; she's raised a hand, not too high, a gesture that detains — "Just a moment" — rather than imperiously signals "Stop." No. The Mercedes rolls to a halt, it has lost its puissance; she seems to be approaching at the same pace.   — Oh can you p'raps lift me again? Thanks so much. —   He does not take in the face at all. He sees only that the road and traffic, in miniature but clear, are reflected across her eyeballs as in one of those convex mirrors at amusement halls.

What could be a more routine incident? A car has stopped and picked up someone who wants to go in the same direction, into town. In less than a minute the action is concluded and the car is moving on with two people in it instead of one.

The driver says — You know me, then? —

— Oh yes. You lifted me and my grandad. You don't remember. —

He listens but what is really holding his attention strangely for a few moments is the wide, flat-topped pyramid of a mine-dump to which he has deliberately turned his gaze as another normal landmark. There: has it not even a certain beauty? There are beautiful, ordinary things left. People say they are unsightly, these dumps, but in some lights . . . This is a firm dump, that the rain has not softened in substance and outline, but that the wonderfully clean sunny air, sluiced by rain, gives at once the clarity of a monument against the glass-blue sky and yet presents curiously as a (remembered) tactile temptation — that whole enormous, regularly-crenellated mountain seems covered with exactly the soft buffed yellow and texture of a much-washed chamois leather. That's it. It is *that* — the imagined sensation of that lovely surface under his hand (the tiny snags of minute hairs when a forearm or backside cheek is brushed against lips) — that produces, unbidden by any thought that normally prompts such an unconscious reaction (God knows, his mind is far enough from these things, this morning) the familiar phenomenon in his body. It's not what the doctor calls a "cold erection" though: pleasureless, something prompted purely by a morbidity in the flesh, what they say happens when a man's hanged. It's more like warmth coming back to a body numbed by cold or shock. Subliminally comforting.

The Conservationist, 1974

Who wouldn't make the world over, if it were easy as that.

—The rise and fall of currencies, of stock exchange prices, of imports and exports, of the supply of labour and the cost of raw materials—

—Of pig-iron.—

—Yes, pig-iron.—

—Ah, I see you do believe in something — you are one of those whose Baal is development—

—What d'you mean, "Baal"?—

—Because you're a pagan, you have to invest some concrete object — a thing — with power outside yourself—

—Coming from a lapsed-Catholic gipsy or whatever it is you are . . . —

She put her hand on him, just under the left pectoral muscle, half patted, half slapped, half caressed. — This is what I believe in — flesh-and-blood people, no gods up in the sky or anywhere on the ground. "Development" — one great big wonderful all-purpose god of a machine, eh, Superjuggernaut that's going to make it all *all right*, put everything right if we just get the finance for it. The money and the know-how machine. Isn't that it, with you? The politics are of no concern. The ideology doesn't matter a damn. The poor devils don't know what's good for them, anyway. That's how you justify what you condone — that's what lets you off the hook, isn't it — the Great Impartial, Development. No dirty hands or compromised minds. Neither dirty racist nor kaffir-boetie. Neither dirty Commie nor Capitalist pig. It's all going to be decided by computer — look, no hands! Change is something programmed, not aspired to. No struggle between human beings. That'd be too smelly and too close. Let them eat cake, by all means — if production allows for it, and dividends are not affected, in time.—

The Conservationist, 1974

The mine-working where Eddie and Vusi hid, that Charles identified as belonging to the turn of the nineteenth century, is in fact far, far older. It goes back further than anything in conventional or alternative history, or even oral tradition, back to the human presences who people anthropology and archaeology, to the hands that shaped the objects or fired the charcoal which may be subjected to carbon tests. No one knows that with the brief occupation of Vusi and Eddie, and the terrible tools that were all they had to work with, a circle was closed; because before the gold-rush prospectors of the 1890s, centuries before time was measured, here, in such units, there was an ancient mine-working out there, and metals precious to men were discovered, dug and smelted, for themselves, by black men.

"Something Out There"
from *Something Out There*, 1984

Steven with bus, Doornfontein, Johannesburg, 1960.

A concession store at Knights, Germiston, 1965. The owners of such stores were granted exclusive rights to trade near the compounds housing a mine's black workers. The bicycle on the roof signifies that the store deals in bicycles.

Nyassa miners going home after serving their twelve-month contract on a gold mine,
Mayfair railway station, Johannesburg, 1952.

9

A barber's chair of mining timbers, near a compound for black miners, Luipaardsvlei Estate Gold Mines, Krugersdorp, 1965.

Bunks in a compound for black miners, Simmer and Jack Gold Mine, Germiston, 1965.

Time Office clerks and a miner, City Deep Gold Mine, Johannesburg, 1966.

Butch Britz, Master Shaftsinker, No. 4 Shaft, President Steyn Gold Mine, Welkom, 1969.

Concession store keepers, Rose Deep Mine, Germiston, 1966.

A company house for a white miner, New Modder, Benoni, 1965.

The Corner House, head office of a mining corporation, Johannesburg, 1965.

A team of Basuto shaftsinkers "lashing" (loading) a kibble at 6,000 feet underground, No. 4 Shaft, President Steyn Gold Mine, Welkom, 1969.

Rose shushes and pushes into the room a little group captured and corralled, bringing with them — a draught from another place and time suddenly blowing through the door — odours that have never been in the house before. Hair ruffles along the small dog's back; one of the grown children quickly and secretly puts a hand on its collar. Smell of wood-smoke, of blankets and clothes stored on mud floors between mud walls that live with the seasons, shedding dust and exuding damp that makes things hatch and sprout; smell of condensed milk, of ashes, of rags saved, of wadded newspapers salvaged, of burning paraffin, of thatch, fowl droppings, leaching red soap, of warm skin and fur, cold earth: the family round the table pause over their meal, its flavour and savour are blown away, the utensils they've been eating with remain in their hands, the presence of a strangeness is out of all proportion to the sight of the black country woman and her children, one close beside her, one on her back. The woman never takes her eyes off Rose, who has set her down there. The baby under the blanket closed over her breast with a giant safety-pin cannot be seen except for a green wool bonnet. Only the small child looks round and round the room; the faces, the table, dishes, glasses, flowers, wine bottle; and seems not to breathe.

"Blinder" from *Something Out There*, 1984

The mists of the night left a vivid freshness that dispels the sickly ammoniacal odour of fowl droppings, the fetid cloying of old thatch, the stinks of rotting garbage —rags, the jaw-bone of a calf, scaly with big glistening flies — that collect wherever the rains have hollowed the ground between huts. Women put out the lengths of cotton they wrap themselves and their babies in. A clear strong sun sweetens the fusty cloth. It glosses the grass roofs and the mud walls change under it to golden ochre; the stuff of which these houses were made is alive.

July's People, 1981

There was a church of mopane and mud with a mopane flagpole to fly a white flag when somebody died; the funeral service was more or less the same Protestant one the missionaries brought from Scotland and it was combined with older rituals to entrust the newly-dead to the ancestors. Ululating women with whitened faces sent them on their way to the missionaries' last judgment. The children were baptized with names chosen by portent in consultation between the mother and an old man who read immutable fate in the fall of small bones cast like dice from a horn cup. On all occasions and most Saturday nights there was a beer-drink, which the chief attended. An upright chair from his house was brought out for him although everyone else squatted comfortably on the sand, and he was offered the first taste from an old decorated gourd dipper (other people drank from baked-bean or pilchard tins) — it is the way of people of the village.

"Oral History" from *A Soldier's Embrace*, 1980

Everything in these villages could be removed at the sweep of a bulldozer or turned to ashes by a single match in the thatch; only the earth, worn to the bone, testified to the permanence of the feet that abraded it, hands that tamped it, hearth-fires that tempered it.

July's People, 1981

Like clouds, the savannah bush formed and re-formed under the changes of light, moved or gave the impression of being moved past by the travelling eye: silent and ashy green as mould spread and always spreading, rolling out under the sky before her. There were hundreds of tracks used since ancient migrations (never ended: her family's was the latest), not seen. There were people, wavering circles of habitation marked by euphorbia and brush hedges, like this one, fungoid fairy rings on grass — not seen. There were cattle cracking through the undergrowth, and the stillness of wild animals — all not to be seen. Space; so confining in its immensity her children did not know it was there.

July's People, 1981

In their houses, there was nothing. At first. You had to
stay in the dark of the hut a long while to make out
what was on the walls. In the wife's hut a wavy pattern of
broad white and ochre bands. In others — she did not
know whether or not she was welcome where they dipped
in and out all day from dark to light like swallows — she
caught a glimpse of a single painted circle, an eye or
target, as she saw it. In one dwelling where she was
invited to enter there was the tail of an animal and a rodent
skull, dried gut, dangling from the thatch. Commonly
there were very small mirrors snapping at the stray beams
of light like hungry fish rising. They reflected nothing.
An impression — sensation — of seeing something
intricately banal, manufactured, replicated, made her
turn as if someone had spoken to her from back there. It
was in the hut where the yokes and traces for the plough-
oxen were. She went inside again and discovered insignia,
like war medals, nailed just to the left of the dark doorway.
The enamel emblem's red cross was foxed and pitted with
damp, bonded with dirt to the mud and dung plaster that
was slowly incorporating it. The engraved lettering on
the brass arm-plaque had filled with rust. The one was a
medallion of the kind presented to black miners who pass
a First Aid exam on how to treat injuries likely to occur
underground, the other was a black miner's badge of
rank, the highest open to him. Someone from the mines;
someone had gone to the gold mines and come home with
these trophies. Or they had been sent home; and where
was the owner? No one lived in this hut. But someone had;
had had possessions, his treasures displayed. Had gone
away, or died — was forgotten or was commemorated by
the evidence of these objects left, or placed, in the hut.
Mine workers had been coming from out of these places
for a long, long time, almost as long as the mines had
existed. She read the brass arm-plaque: BOSS BOY.

July's People, 1981

A peasant woman at home, Coffee Bay, Transkei, 1975.

25

The house of a couple who had gone to Cape Town to look for work, Engcobo, Transkei, 1975.

The peasant woman's oil lamp, Coffee Bay, Transkei, 1975.

Forest and huts near Coffee Bay, Transkei, 1975.

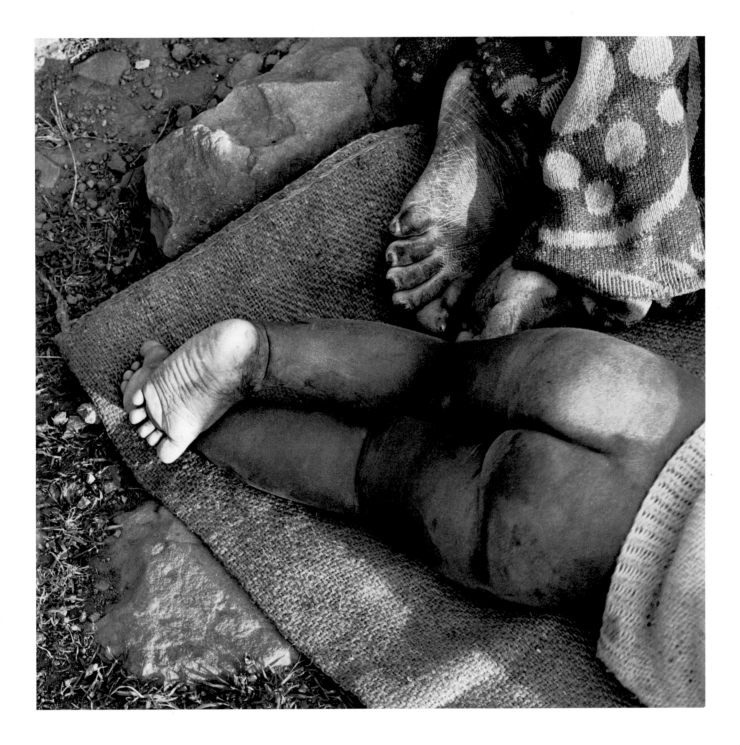

Grandmother and child, Transkei, 1975.

Circumcision initiate in the hut of the initiates, Pondoland, 1975.

"Boss Boy," Battery Reef, Randfontein Estates Gold Mine, 1966. In right pocket: tobacco pouch. In left pocket: clinometer for underground measurements and notebook for recording them. On left arm: company rank badge with three stars to indicate Mine Overseer's Boss Boy. On right wrist: company identity band. On belt: pocketknife in homemade sheath, Zobo watch presented by company in recognition of accident-free work, and first-aid kit.

I went with Steven into the townships, the shebeens, the rooms and houses of his friends. I do not want to suggest by this a descent into an underworld, but another world, in which the conditions of the Johannesburg I worked and lived in did not pertain. First, the scale of proportion was reversed: in the city, and in my suburban street, the buildings rose above, the gardens made a space around the people — we lived, as city people do, in the shelter of the city, in a context that, while overshadowing, also provides the dignity of concealment: figures in the street pass out of sight under trees and shadows, living passes out of sight behind walls and fences. By contrast, an African township looked like something that had been razed almost to the ground. The mass of houses and shacks were so low and crowded together that the people seemed to be swarming over them, as if they had just invaded a deserted settlement. Every time I went to a township I was aware of this sudden drop in the horizon of buildings and rise of humans — nothing concealed, nothing sheltered, in any but the most obvious sense, any moment of the people's lives. A blinding light of reality never left them. And they lived, all the time, in all the layers of society at once: pimps, gangsters, errand boys, washwomen, schoolteachers, boxers, musicians and under-takers, labourers, and patent medicine men — these were neighbours, and shared a tap, a yard, even a lavatory.

A World of Strangers, 1958

The location is like the dump; the children do not know what there is to find there, either. It is not at all like the farm, where what you will find is birds' eggs, wire, or something (a coin, a pocket comb, cigar stumps) white people have dropped or thrown away. A ring was lost; the children were told to look for a shiny stone in the grass. Once there was a tortoise, and the parents ate it and the shell is still in Jacobus's house.

They roamed the streets of the location seeing into houses that had furniture, like the white farmer's house, and peach trees fenced in, with dogs like the India's barking, and they passed other kinds of houses, long rows of rooms marked off into separate dwellings by the pink and blue paint used on the exterior, where a lot of men from the factories lived and made mounds of beer cartons on the waste ground around. Outside a hall as big as a church they saw the huge coloured pictures of white men shooting each other or riding horses but they had never paid to go inside. They went into little shops like the India's and bought five cents' hot chips wetted with vinegar, and hung about against the glass walls of the biggest store in the location with thousands of different coloured bottles of liquor behind its fancy steel burglar grilles. They saw men in clothes better than anything Izak had, white caps and sunglasses, wonderful watches and rings on hands resting on coloured fur-covered steering wheels of cars. There were women wearing the straight hair of white people and hospital nurses in uniforms clean and stiff as paper. There was an abundance of the rarities carefully saved, on the farm: everybody here had boxes and carriers and bottles and plastic cans in their hands or on their heads. A child had a little three-wheeled bicycle; a shopkeeper chased a screaming girl who had taken a pineapple. They played in the streets with some children who suddenly snatched their chips off them and disappeared; a balloon was handed to them from a van with a voice like Izak's radio, telling people to buy medicine for their blood. Looking on at boys their own age gambling they saw one pull a knife and thrust it into the back of the other's hand. They ran. But they went back; always they went back. One had once been farther, actually into Johannesburg, lying on a manure hawker's cart and seeing the buildings, enormous, jolting all round as if about to topple with the movement of the frightened horse and uneven axles in the traffic.

Walking home after school from the location, the dirt road gathered itself ahead or behind, rolling up its surface into a great charge of dust coming at them; there was a moment when they saw a car and a face or faces at the fuming centre, and then they were whipped into turmoil, it lashed round them a furry tongue of fiery soft dust spitting stinging chips of stone. When they could breathe and see again, the fury was already gathering up the road on the other side, smoking against the sun and blocking the other horizon.

The Conservationist, 1974

She was sitting in the yard with him and his friends the Sunday a cousin arrived with a couple of hangers-on. They didn't bring beer, but were given some. There were greetings, but who really hears names? One of the hangers-on fell asleep on the grass, a boy with a body like a baggy suit. The other had a yellow face, lighter than anyone else present, narrow as a trowel, and the irregular pock-marks of the pitted skin were flocked, round the area where men grow hair, with sparse tufts of black. She noticed he wore a gold ear-ring in one ear. He had nothing to say but later took up a guitar belonging to someone else and played to himself. One of the people living in the garage, crossing the path of the group under the arbour on his way to the lavatory with his roll of toilet paper, paused to look or listen, but everyone else was talking too loudly to hear the soft plang-plang, and the after-buzz when the player's palm stilled the instrument's vibration.

Moreke went off with his friends when they left, and came back, not late. His wife had gone to bed. She was sleepy, feeding the baby. Because he stood there, at the foot of the bed, did not begin to undress, she understood someone must be with him.

"Mtembu's friend." Her husband's head indicated the other side of the glass-paned door.

"What does he want here now?"

"I brought him. Mtembu asked."

"What for?"

Moreke sat down on the bed. He spoke softly, mouthing at her face. "He needs somewhere to stay."

"Where was he before, then?"

Moreke lifted and dropped his elbows limply at a question not to be asked.

The baby lost the nipple and nuzzled furiously at air. She guided its mouth. "Why can't he stay with Mtembu. You could have told Mtembu no."

"He's your cousin."

"Well, I will tell him no. If Mtembu needs somewhere to stay, I have to take him. But not anyone he brings from the street."

Her husband yawned, straining every muscle in his face. Suddenly he stooped and began putting together the sheets of his Sunday paper that were scattered on the floor. He folded them more or less in order, slapping and smoothing the creases.

"Well?"

He said nothing, walked out. She heard the voices in the kitchen, but not what was being said.

He opened their door again and shut it behind him. "It's not a business of cousins. This one is in trouble. You don't read the papers . . . the blowing up of that police station . . . *you* know, last month? They didn't catch them all . . . It isn't safe for Mtembu to keep him any longer. He must keep moving."

Her soft jowls stiffened.

Her husband assured her awkwardly. "A few days. Only for a couple of days. Then — (a gesture) — out of the country."

"A City of the Dead, A City of the Living"
from *Something Out There*, 1984

That night the two men didn't talk. They seemed to have nothing to say. Like prisoners who get their last mealie-pap of the day before being locked up for the night, Moreke's wife gave them their meal before dark. Then all three went from the kitchen to the Morekes' room, where any light that might shine from behind the curtains and give away a presence was directed only towards a blind: a high corrugated tin fence in a lane full of breast-high khakiweed. Moreke shared his newspaper. When the man had read it, he tossed through third-hand adventure comics and the sales promotion pamphlets given away in city supermarkets Nanike Moreke kept; he read the manual "Teach Yourself How to Sell Insurance" in which, at some stage, "Samson Moreke" had been carefully written on the fly-leaf.

There was no beer. Moreke's wife knew her way about her kitchen in the dark; she fetched the litre bottle of Coke that was on the kitchen table and poured herself a glass. Her husband stayed the offer with a raised hand; the other man's inertia over the manual was overcome just enough to move his head in refusal. She had taken up again the cover for the bed she had begun when she had had some free time, waiting for this fifth child to be born. Crocheted roses, each caught in a squared web of a looser pattern, were worked separately and then joined to the whole they slowly extended. The tiny flash of her steel hook and the hair-thin gold in his ear signalled in candlelight. At about ten o'clock there was a knock at the front door. The internal walls of these houses are planned at minimum specification for cheapness and a blow on any part of the house reverberates through every room. The black-framed, bone-yellow face raised and held, absolutely still, above the manual. Moreke opened his mouth and, swinging his legs over the side, lifted himself from the bed. But his wife's hand on his shoulder made him subside again; only the bed creaked slightly. The slenderness of her body from the waist up was merely rooted in heavy maternal hips and thighs; with a movement soft as the breath she expelled, she leant and blew out the candles.

"A City of the Dead, A City of the Living"
from *Something Out There*, 1984

35

On Saturday Moreke took his blue ruled pad and an envelope to the kitchen table. But his wife was peeling pumpkin and slicing onions, there was no space, so he went back to the room where the sofa was, and his radio-and-cassette-player. First he addressed the envelope to their twelve-year-old boy at mission school. It took him the whole morning to write a letter, although he could read so well. Once or twice he asked the man how to spell a word in English.

He lay smoking on his bed, the sofa. "Why in English?"

"Rapula knows English very well . . . it helps him to get letters . . ."

"You shouldn't send him away from here, *baba*. You think it's safer, but you are wrong. It's like you and the meetings. The more you try to be safe, the worse it will be for your children."

He stared quietly at Moreke. "And look, now I'm here."

"Yes."

"And you look after me."

"Yes."

"And you're not afraid."

"Yes, we're afraid . . . but of many things . . . when I come home with money . . . Three times tsotsis have hit me, taken everything. You see here where I was cut on the cheek. This arm was broken. I couldn't work. Not even push the lawnmower. I had to pay some young one to hold my jobs for me."

The man smoked and smiled. "I don't understand you. You see? I don't understand you. Bring your children home, man. We're shut up in the ghetto to kill each other. That's what they want, in their white city. So you send the children away; that's what they want, too. To get rid of us. We must all stick together. That's the only way to fight our way out."

"A City of the Dead, A City of the Living"
from *Something Out There*, 1984

36

Mofolo South, Soweto, 1972.

Cup Final, Orlando Stadium, Soweto, 1972.

George and Sarah Manyani at home, Emdeni Extension, Soweto, 1972.

Ephraim Zulu watering his garden, Central Western Jabavu, Soweto, 1972.

40

Butchering the horse of a coal merchant for the sale of its meat, Tladi, Soweto, 1972.

Sunset over the playing fields of Tladi, Soweto, 1972.

42

Margaret Mcingana at home on a Sunday afternoon, Zola Soweto, 1970.

They would be standing under the trees, the corseted women, the thin, gracious women who always dressed as if for a garden party, the satellite young daughters in pastel frocks. Where the drinks were, the men would be, faces red from golf and bowls, voices loud, laughing and expansive in departmental allusions as cosy as family jokes; the older men spry or corpulent with position, the up-and-coming younger men showing here a hinted thickness of neck, there a knee peaking up bony which assured that when the first lot died off, the second would be ready to replace them identically. As the darkness tangled with the trees, and the boys "borrowed" from the office or Compound brought the braziers to the right stage of glow, the daughters and the young sons would stand well away to avoid splashing their light frocks and blue suits and patent-leather shoes while they roasted lamb chops stuck on long forks. The smell of hair oil and lavender water would come out in the heat, mixed with the smoke and acridity of burning fat. They would giggle and lick their fingers, eating with the small bites of mice. And run over the lawns back to the house to wash their hands and come back, waving handkerchiefs freshly charged with lavender water. I had been there many times. I knew what it was like; a small child in white party shoes that made my feet big and noisy, tearing in and out among the grownups, wild with the excitement of the fire and the smoky dark; and then grown up myself, standing first on one foot, then the other, drawing patterns with my toe on the ground, feebly part of the feebleness of it all, the mawkish attempts of the boys to entertain, the inane response of the girls: the roasting of meat to be torn apart by hands and teeth made as feeble as a garden party. That was what these people did to everything in life; enfeebled it. Weddings were the appearance of dear little girls dressed up to strew rose petals, rather than matings; death was the speculation about who would step up to the dead man's position; dignity was the chain of baubles the mayor wore round his neck.

The Lying Days, 1953

I sat there behind the swag of carnations and roses that decorated the bride's table, eating smoked salmon and drinking champagne, and felt only an empathetic inward trill of shyness — hidden by the smile politely exchanged with the uncle next to me — when Max got up to speak. Max is — was — slight and not very tall, but he had the big wrists and the small bright blue, far-sighted eyes of his mother's antecedents; in him, unmistakably, was the Boer identity that she archly claimed for herself. He wore his dark suit and his best, raw silk tie that I had given him. He gave, to the expanse of tablecloth directly beneath him rather than anywhere else, the nervous smile that always reminded me of the mouth-movement of an uncertain feline animal, not snarling, unable to express a greeting, yet acknowledging an approach. He did not look at me, nor at anyone. His first few words were lost in the talk that had not quite yet damped down, but then his voice emerged, ". . . my sister and Allan, the man she has chosen to marry, a happy life together. Naturally we wish them this, though there's not much more we can do about it than wish. I mean it's up to them."

There was a stir towards laughter, a false start — they were expecting to have to respond to a joke or innuendo soon, but Max did not seem to understand, and went on, "I don't know Allan at all, and although I think I know my sister, I don't suppose I know much about her, either. We have to leave it to them to make a go of it for themselves. And — good luck to them. They're young, my sister's beautiful—"

And this time the growl of laughter was confident. Max became inaudible, though I guessed he was probably saying something about the beauty being in spite of the way she'd been got up for the day. The guests had decided that his ignoring of their response was some sort of dead-pan wit and their laughter surged appreciatively into every pause or hesitation as he went on, ". . . between the two of them. But the kind of life they'll live, the way they'll live among other people — that's another thing again, and here one can have something to say. I know I'm supposed to be speaking for everybody here " (there was an emotional murmur of support) "— all these people who have know Queen since she was born, and who have known her husband, known Allan — and who have come here full of the good feeling they get when they get together and drink each other's health — your health, Queen and Allan — but I'd like to say off my own bat" (eyes were on him with the indulgent, smiling attention good manners decreed) "don't let the world begin and end for you with the—how many is it? four hundred?—people sitting here in this — the Donnybrook Country *and Sporting* Club today. These good friends of our parents

and Allan's parents, our father's regional chairman and the former ministers of this and that (I don't want to make a mistake in the portfolios) and all the others, I don't know the names but I recognize the faces, all right — who have made us, and made this club, and made this country what it is." (There was prolonged clapping, led by someone with loud, hard palms.) "There's a whole world outside this." (Applause broke out again.) "Shut outside. Kept out. Shutting this in . . . Don't stay inside and let your arteries harden, like theirs . . . I'm not talking about the sort of thing some of them have, those who have had their thrombosis, I don't mean veins gone furry through sitting around in places like this fine club and having more than enought to eat — " (Clapping began and spattered out, like mistaken applause between movements at a concert) "What I'm asking you to look out for is — is moral sclerosis. Moral sclerosis. Hardening of the heart, narrowing of the mind; while the dividends go up. The thing that makes them distribute free blankets in the Location in winter, while refusing to pay wages people could live on. Smugness. Among us, you can't be too young to pick it up. It sets in pretty quick. More widespread than bilharzia in the rivers, and a damned side harder to cure."

There was a murmurous titter. The uncle beside me whispered anxiously, "He's inherited his father's gifts as a speaker."

"It's a hundred-per-cent endemic in places like this Donnybrook Country *and Sporting* Club, and in all the suburbs you're likely to choose from to live in. Just don't be too sure they're healthy, our nice clean suburbs for whites only."

They were smiling blindly, deafly, keeping their attitudes of bland attention as they would have done if the hostess had lost her panties on the dance floor, or they had suddenly overheard an embarrassing private noise.

"— and your children. If you have babies, Queenie and Allan, don't worry too much about who kisses them — it's what they'll tell them, later, that infects. It's what being nicely brought up will make of them that you've got to watch out for. Moral sclerosis — yes, that's all I wanted to say, just stay alive and feeling and thinking — and that's all I can say that'll be of any use . . ."

Max suddenly became aware of the people about him, and sat down. There was a second of silence and then the same pair of hard palms began to clap and a few other hands followed hollowly, but someone at the bride's table at once leapt up and thrust out his glass in the toast that Max had forgotten — "The bride and groom!"

The Late Bourgeois World, 1966

Mrs Lily Scholtz was hanging on the line the lilac nylon capes the clients of "Chez Lily," her hairdressing salon, are given to wear, and which she brings home to pop into the washing machine every Sunday. Her husband, Bokkie, former mining shift-boss turned car salesman, was helping their neighbour with the vehicle he is building for drag racing. Mrs Scholtz heard the dustbin lid clang and thought her cat, named after a TV series Mrs Scholtz hadn't missed an episode of, some years back, was in there again. The dustbin is kept between the garage and the maid's room where Bokkie Scholtz does carpentry — his hobby; Patience Ngulungu doesn't live in, but comes to work from Naledi Township weekdays only. Mrs Scholtz found the lid off the bin but no sign of Dallas. As she bent to replace the lid, something landed on her back and bit her just below the right shoulder. Out of nowhere — as she was to relate many times. First thing she knew, there was this terrible pain, as if her arm were torn off — but it wasn't; without even realizing that she did it, she had swung back with that same arm, holding the metal lid, at what had bitten her, just as you swat wildly at a bee. She did not hit anything; when she turned round there it was — she saw a big grey monkey already up on the roof of the garage. It was gibbering and she was screaming, Bokkie, Bokkie.

Mr Bokkie Scholtz said his blood ran cold. You know what Johannesburg is like these days. They are everywhere, loafers, illegals, robbers, murderers, the pass laws are a joke, you can't keep them out of white areas. He was over the wall from his neighbour's place and took the jump into his own yard, God knows how he didn't break a leg. And there she was with blood running down and a big grey baboon on the roof. (His wife refers to all these creatures as monkeys.) The thing was chattering, its lips curled back to show long fangs — that's what it'd sunk into her shoulder, teeth about an inch-and-a-half long —can you imagine? He just wanted to get his wife safely out of the way, that's all. He pushed her into the kitchen and ran for his shotgun. When he got back to the yard, it was still on the roof (must have shinned up by the drainpipe, and to come down that way would have brought it

right to Bokkie Scholtz's feet). He fired, but was in such a state, you can imagine — hands shaking — missed the head and got the bastard in the arm — funny thing, almost the same place it had bitten Lily. And then, would you believe it, one arm hanging useless, it ran round to the other side of the garage roof and took a leap — ten feet it must be —right over to that big old tree they call a Tree of Heaven, in the neighbour's garden on the other side. Of course he raced next door and he and the neighbours were after it, but it got away, from tree to tree (their legs are like another pair of arms), up that steep little street that leads to the koppies of Kensington Ridge, and he never had the chance of another shot at it.

The Bokkie Scholtzs' house is burglar-proofed, has fine wires on windows and doors which activate an alarm that goes hysterical, with noises like those science fiction films have taught come from outer space, whenever Dallas tries to get in through a fanlight. They have a half-breed Rottweiler who was asleep, apparently, on the front stoep, when the attack came. It just shows you — whatever you do, you can't call yourself safe.

"Something Out There"
from *Something Out There*, 1984

Yet although the lovely home was every brick as good as any modern lovely home in the city, it had something of the enclosing gloom of the farmhouse in which Naas had spent his childhood. He never brought that childhood to the light of reminiscence or reflection because he had put all behind him: he was on the other side of the divide history had opened between the farmer and the trader, the past when the Boers were a rural people and the *uitlanders* ran commerce, and the present, when the Afrikaners governed an industrialized state and had become entrepreneurs, stockbrokers, beer millionaires — all the synonyms for traders. When he began to plan the walls to house his wife's artistic ideas, a conception of dimness, long gaunt passages by which he had been contained at his Ma's place, and his Ouma's, loomed its proportions around the ideas.

"Something Out There"
from *Something Out There*, 1984

Sarah worked for us before her legs got too bad. She was very fat, and her skin was light yellow-brown, as if, like a balloon that lightens in colour as it is blown up, the fat swelling beneath the thin layer of pigment caused it to stretch and spread more and more sparsely. She wore delicate little gilt-rimmed spectacles and she was a good cook, though extravagant with butter.

"Ah, Woe Is Me" from *Selected Stories*, 1976

Property developers' billboard, Sunward Park, Boksburg, 1980.

House with concrete fence, Sunward Park, Boksburg, 1980.

A maid on Abel Road, Hillbrow, Johannesburg, 1973.

51

Dining room detail, Randburg, 1974.

Girl in her new tutu on the stoep of her parents' house, Boksburg, 1980.

In the mayor's parlour, at the Town Hall, Boksburg, 1980.

Ballroom dancing teacher Ted Van Rensburg watches two of his pupils swinging to the music of Victor
Sylvester and His Orchestra in the old Court House, Boksburg, 1980.

By the time they went in, they were free of the evening. Her black dress, her ear-rings and her bracelets felt like fancy-dress; she shed the character and sat on the bedroom carpet, and, passing her, he said "Oh — that chap of Flora's came today, but I don't think he'll last. I explained to him that I didn't have the sort of job he was looking for."

"Well, that's all right, then," she said inquiringly. "What more could you do?"

"Yes," he said, deprecating. "But I could see he didn't like the idea much. It's a cleaner's job; nothing for him. He's an intelligent chap. I didn't like having to offer it to him."

She was moving about her dressing table, piling out upon it the contents of her handbag. "Then I'm sure he'll understand. It'll give him something for the time being, anyway, darling. You can't help it if you don't need the sort of work he does."

"Huh, he won't last. I could see that. He accepted it, but only with his head. He'll get fed up. Probably won't turn up tomorrow. I had to speak to him about his Congress button, too. The works manager came to me."

"What about his Congress button?" she said.

He was unbuttoning his shirt and his eyes were on the unread evening paper that lay folded on the bed. "He was wearing one," he said inattentively.

"I know, but what did you have to speak to him about it for?"

"He was wearing it in the workshop all day."

"Well, what about it?" She was sitting at her dressing table, legs spread, as if she had sat heavily and suddenly. She was not looking at him, but at her own face.

He gave the paper a push and drew his pyjamas from under the pillow. Vulnerable and naked, he said authoritatively, "You can't wear a button like that among the men in the workshop."

"Good heavens," she said, almost in relief, laughing, backing away from the edge of tension, chivvying him out of a piece of stuffiness. "And why can't you?"

"You can't have someone clearly representing a political organization like Congress."

"But he's not there *representing* anything, he's there as a workman?" Her mouth was still twitching with something between amusement and nerves.

"Exactly."

"Then why can't he wear a button that signifies his allegiance to an organization in his private life outside the workshop? There's no rule about not wearing tie-pins or club buttons or anything, in the workshop, is there?"

"No, there isn't, but that's not quite the same thing."

"My dear William," she said, "it is exactly the same.

It's nothing to do with the works manager whether a man wears a Rotary button, or an Elvis Presley button, or an African National Congress button. It's damn all his business."

"No, Madge, I'm sorry," William said, patient, "but it's not the same. I can give the man a job because I feel sympathetic towards the struggle he's in, but I can't put him in the workshop as a Congressman. I mean, that wouldn't be fair to Fowler. That I can't do to Fowler." He was smiling as he went towards the bathroom, but his profile, as he turned into the doorway, was incisive.

She sat on at her dressing-table, pulling a comb through her hair, dragging it down through knots. Then she rested her face on her palms, caught sight of herself and became aware, against her fingers, of the curving shelf of bone, like the lip of a strong shell, under each eye. Everyone has his own intimations of mortality. For her, the feel of the bone beneath the face, in any living creature, brought her the message of the skull. Once hollowed out of this, outside the world, too. For what it's worth. It's worth a lot, the world, she affirmed, as she always did, life rising at once in her as a fish opens its jaws to a fly. It's worth a lot; and she sighed and got up with the sigh.

She went into the bathroom and sat down on the edge of the bath. He was lying there in the water, his chin relaxed on his chest, and he smiled at her. She said, "You mean you don't want Fowler to know."

"Oh," he said, seeing where they were again. "What is it I don't want Fowler to know?"

"You don't want your partner to know that you slip black men with political ideas into your workshop. Cheeky kaffir agitators. Specially a man who's been in jail for getting people to defy the government! — What was his name; you never said?"

"Daniel something. I don't know. Mongoma or Ngoma. Something like that."

A line like a cut appeared between her eyebrows. "Why can't you remember his name?" Then she went on at once, "You don't want Fowler to know what you think, do you? That's it? You want to pretend you're like him, you don't mind the native in his place. You want to pretend that to please Fowler. You don't want Fowler to think you're cracked or Communist or whatever it is that good-natured, kind, jolly rich people like old Fowler think about people like us."

"I couldn't have less interest in what Fowler thinks outside our boardroom. And inside it, he never thinks about anything but how to sell more earth-moving gear."

"I don't mind the native in his place. You want him to think you go along with all that." She spoke aloud, but she seemed to be telling herself rather than him.

"Fowler and I run a factory. Our only common interest is the efficient running of that factory. Our *only* one. The factory depends on a stable, satisfied black labour-force, and that we've got. Right, you and I know that the whole black wage standard is too low, right, we know that they haven't a legal union to speak for them, right, we know that the conditions they live under make it impossible for them really to be stable. All that. But the fact is, so far as accepted standards go in this crazy country, they're a stable, satisfied labour-force with better working conditions than most. So long as I'm a partner in a business that lives by them, I can't officially admit an element that represents dissatisfaction with their lot."

"A green badge with a map of Africa on it," she said.

"If you make up your mind not to understand, you don't, and there it is," he said indulgently.

"You give him a job but you make him hide his Congress button."

He began to soap himself. She wanted everything to stop while she inquired into things, she could not go on while a remark was unexplained or a problem unsettled, but he represented a principle she subscribed to but found so hard to follow, that life must go on, trivially, commonplace, the trailing hem of the only power worth clinging to. She smoothed the film of her nightgown over the shape of her knees, over and over, and presently she said, in exactly the flat tone of statement that she had used before, the flat tone that was the height of belligerence in her, "He can say and do what he likes, he can call for strikes and boycotts and anything he likes, outside the factory, but he mustn't wear his Congress button at work."

He was standing up, washing his body that was full of scars; she knew them all, from the place on his left breast where a piece of shrapnel had gone in, all the way back to the place under his arm where he had torn himself on barbed wire as a child. "Yes, of course, anything he likes."

"Anything except his self-respect," she grumbled to herself. "Pretend, pretend. Pretend he doesn't belong to a political organization. Pretend he doesn't want to be a man. Pretend he hasn't been to prison for what he believes." Suddenly she spoke to her husband: "You'll let him have anything except the one thing worth giving."

"Something for the Time Being"
from *Selected Stories*, 1976

He was born in the townships and had never lived the traditional African life of raising crops and herding cattle, neither had he known the city white child's attachment to a pastoral ancestry fostered from an early age by the traditional "treats" of picnics and camping. He belonged to town life in a way that no white man does in a country where it is any white man's privilege to have the leisure and money to get out into the veld or down to the beaches.

Occasion for Loving, 1963

The hard twist of excreta was plaited with fur and sinew: Charles picked it up in his bare hand. —See that? It had rabbit for supper. A jackal.—

Joy gave a shivery laugh, although there was no prowling man to fear. —So close to the house?—

Vusi was disbelieving. —Nothing to eat there. — The converted shed with its roll-down metal door was just behind them.

—Well, they pad around, sniff around. I suppose this place's still got a whiff of chickens and pigs. It's quite common even now, you get the odd jackal roaming fairly near to towns.—

—Are you sure? How can you know it's jackal, Charlie?—

Charles waggled the dung under Eddie's nose.

—Hey, man!— Eddie backed off, laughing nervously.

Vusi was a tester of statements rather than curious. —Can you tell all kinds of animals' business?—

—Of course. First there's the shape and size, that's easy, ay, anyone can tell an elephant's from a bird's— They laughed, but Charles was matter-of-fact, as someone who no longer works in a factory will pick up a tool and use it with the same automative skill learnt on an assembly line. —But even if the stuff is broken up, you can say accurately which animal by examining food content. The bushmen — the San, Khoikhoi — they've practiced it for centuries, part of their hunting skills.—

—Is that what they taught you at Scouts, man?—

—No. Not Scouts exactly.—

—So where'd you pick it up?— Eddie rallied the others. —A Number Two expert! He's clever, old Charlie. We're lucky to have a chap like him, ay!—

Joy was listening politely, half-smiling, to Charles retelling, laconically self-censored, what had been the confidences of their early intimacy.

—Once upon a time I was a game ranger, believe it or not.— That was one of the things he had tried in order to avoid others: not to have to go into metal and corrugated paper packaging in which his father and uncles held forty per cent of the shares, not to take up (well, all right, if you're not cut out for business) an opening in a quasi-governmental fuel research unit — without, for a long

58

time, knowing that there was no way out for him, neither the detachment of science nor the consolations of nature. Born what he was, where he was, knowing what he knew, outrage would have burned down to shame if he had thought his generation had any right left to something in the careers guide.

—You're kidding. Where?—

—Oh, around. An ignoramus with a B.Sc. Honours, but the Shangaan rangers educated me.—

—Oh, Kruger Park, you mean. They work there. That place.—Vusi's jerk of the head cut off his words like an appalled flick of fingers. Once, he had come in through the vast wilderness of protected species; an endangered one on his way to become operational. Fear came back to him as a layer of cold liquid under the scalp. All that showed was that his small stiff ears pulled slightly against his skull.

Charles wiped his palm on his pants and clasped hands behind his head, easing his neck, his matronly pectorals flexing to keep in trim while waiting. —One day I'd like to apply the methodology to humans — a class *analy*sis. (He enjoyed their laughter.) The sewage from a white suburb and the sewage from a squatters' camp — you couldn't find a better way of measuring the level of sustenance afforded by different income levels, even the snobbery imposed by different occupations and aspirations. A black street-sweeper who scoffed half a loaf and a Bantu beer for lunch, a white executive who's digested oysters and a bottle of Fleur du Cap — show me what you shit, man, and I'll tell you who you are.—

"Something Out There"
from *Something Out There*, 1984

At night Eddie and Vusi lay low on their mattresses in a perspective that enclosed them with boxes and packing cases like a skyline of children's piled blocks. Eddie slept quickly but Vusi, with his shaved head with the tiny, gristly ears placed at exactly the level of the cheekbones that stretched his face and formed the widest plane of the whole skull, lay longing to smoke. Yet the craving was just another appetite, some petty recurrence, assuaged a thousand times and easily to be so again with something bought across a corner shop counter. Around him in the dark, an horizon darker than the dark held the cold forms in which the old real, terrible needs of his life, his father's life, and his father's father's life were now so strangely realized. He had sat at school farting the gases of an empty stomach, he had seen fathers, uncles, brothers, come home without work from days-long queues, he had watched, too young to understand, the tin and board that had been the shack he was born in, carted away by government demolishers. His bare feet had been shod in shoes worn to the shape of a white child's feet. He had sniffed glue to see a rosy future. He had taken a diploma by correspondence to better himself. He had spoken nobody's name under interrogation. He had left a girl and baby without hope of being able to show himself to them again. You could not eat the AKM assault rifles that Charles had brought in golf-bags, you could not dig a road or turn a lathe with the limpet mines, could not shoe and clothe feet and body with the offensive and defensive hand grenades, could not use the AKM bayonets to compete with the white man's education, or to thrust a way out of solitary confinement in maximum security, and the wooden boxes that held hundreds of rounds of ammunition would not make even a squatter's shack for the girl and child.

"Something Out There"
from *Something Out There*, 1984

Meeting of the worker-management liaison committee of the
Colgate Palmolive Company, Boksburg, 1980.

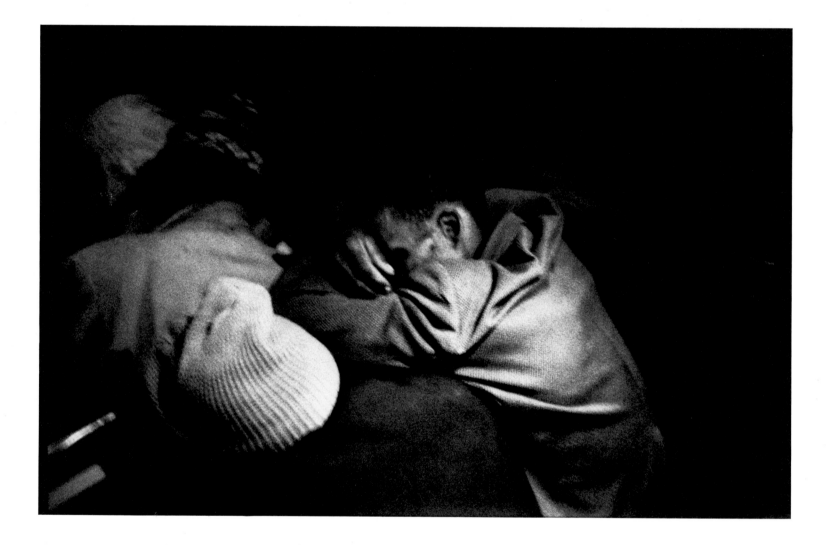

Busing to work: 4:00 a.m. on the 2:30 a.m. bus from Wolwerkraal, in KwaNdebele, to Marabastad, in Pretoria; one and a half hours still to go. 1983.

Busing from work: 8:45 p.m. on the 7:00 p.m. bus from Marabastad to Waterval; forty-five minutes still to go. The people of KwaNdebele, most of whom were compulsorily settled there in pursuance of apartheid policy, need to travel between two and eight hours per day simply to get to work in Pretoria and back to their homes in the resettlement camps of KwaNdebele. 1984.

Young men with "pass" book. Any black person without a valid pass in his possession was liable to summary arrest. White City, Jabavu, Soweto, 1972.

No work, no pass, no legal rights to employment or residence in the area in which they have been "settled," a family in their shelter at KTC Squatter Camp, Cape Town. Their shelter had been demolished by officials of the Western Cape Development Board more times than they could remember—perhaps thirty or forty times, they thought. 1984.

Plastic shelters, KTC Squatter Camp, Cape Town, 1984.

J. J. Oosthuizen of the West Rand Development Board and Senior Township Superintendent Senoane,
Soweto, 1972.

These houses I was coming to had a pattern all over them marked into the mud they were built of. There was a mound of dried cows' business, as tall as I was, stacked up in a pattern, too. And then the usual junk our people have, just like in the Location: old tins, broken things collected from white people's rubbish heaps. The fowls ran sideways from my feet and two old men let their talking die away into ahas and ehês as I came up. I greeted them the right way to greet old men and they nodded and went on ehêing and ahaing to show that they had been greeted properly. One of them had very clean ragged trousers tied with string and he sat on the ground, but the other, sitting on a bucket-seat that must have been taken from some scrapyard car, was dressed in a way I've never seen — from the old days, I suppose. He wore a black suit with very wide trousers, laced boots, a stiff white collar and black tie, and on top of it all, a broken old hat. It was Sunday, of course, so I suppose he was all dressed up. I've heard that these people who work for farmers wear sacks most of the time. The old ones didn't ask me what I wanted there. They just peered at me with their eyes gone the colour of soapy water because they were so old. And I didn't know what to say because I hadn't thought what I was going to say, I'd just walked. Then a little kid slipped out of the dark doorway quick as a cockroach. I thought perhaps everyone else was out because it was Sunday but then a voice called from inside the other house, and when the child didn't answer, called again, and a woman came to the doorway.

I said my bicycle had a puncture and could I have some water.

She said something into the house and in a minute a girl, about fifteen she must've been, edged past her carrying a paraffin tin and went off to fetch water. Like all the girls that age, she never looked at you. Her body shook under an ugly old dress and she almost hobbled in her hurry to get away. Her head was tied up in a rag-doek right down to the eyes the way old-fashioned people do, otherwise she would have been quite pretty, like any other girl. When she had gone a little way the kid went pumping after her, panting, yelling, opening his skinny legs wide as scissors over stones and antheaps, and then he caught up with her and you could see that right away she was quite different, I knew how it was, she yelled at him, you heard her laughter as she chased him with the tin, whirled around from out of his clutching hands, struggled with him; they were together like Emma and I used to be when we got away from the old lady, and from the school, and everybody. And Emma was also one of our girls who have the big strong comfortable bodies of mothers even when they're still kids, maybe it comes from always lugging the smaller one round on their backs.

"Some Monday for Sure" from *Selected Stories*, 1976

That's the trouble when you work alone in an office, like I do, you don't make friends at your work. Nobody to talk to but those duckies in the workshop, and what can I have in common with a lot of louts in black leather jackets? No respect, either, you should hear the things they come out with. I'd sooner talk to the blacks, that's the truth, though I know it sounds a strange thing to say. At least they call you missus. Even old Madala knows he can't come into my office without taking his cap off, though heaven help you if you ask that boy to run up to the Greek for a packet of smokes, or round to the Swiss Confectionary. I had a dust-up with him once over it, the old monkey-face, but the manager didn't seem to want to get rid of him, he's been here so long. So he just keeps out of my way and he has his half-crown from me at Christmas, same as the other boys. But you get more sense out of the boss-boy, Jack, than you can out of some whites, believe me, and he can make you laugh, too, in his way — of course they're like children, you see them yelling with laughter over something in their own language, noisy lot of devils; I don't suppose we'd think it funny at all if we knew what it was all about. This Jack used to get a lot of phone calls (I complained to the manager on the quiet and he's put a stop to it, now) and the natives on the other end used to be asking to speak to Mpanza and Makiwane and I don't know what all, and when I'd say there wasn't anyone of that name working here they'd come out with it and ask for Jack. So I said to him one day, "Why do you people have a hundred and one names, why don't these uncles and aunts and brothers-in-law come out with your name straight away and stop wasting my time?" He said, "Here I'm Jack because Mpanza Makiwane is not a name, and there I'm Mpanza Makiwane because Jack is not a name, but I'm the only one who knows who I am where ever I am."

"Good Climate, Friendly Inhabitants"
from *Selected Stories*, 1976

She must have drawn breath as she heard the door open, for she said at once, from the top of her chest and the back of her distended nostrils, "Mr Hood, 'ev yoo brought natives into the bullding. I'v hed complaints yoo been bringing natives in the bullding, end jis now Mr Jarvis seen yoo coming in the front door with natives."

I said, "Yes, Mrs Jarvis?" standing there with the glass in my hand as if I were about to propose a toast.

She came past me into the hall and closed the door. I guessed that she was not fully dressed beneath her fur coat; she held it tightly around her all the time. "I wanna tell yoo, Mr Hood, whatever yoo been used to, this is'n a location, yoo can't 'ev natives. If yoo bringing natives, yoo'll 'ev to go." Her breath was quite expelled. She looked past me as if she could not bring herself to look at me. She was a very clean, overdressed, overpainted woman, and now, just as always when she passed you on the stairs, she smelled of cigarettes and toilet soap.

"I can have whom I please in my own flat so long as I pay the rent."

Through the open door into my room, she saw Peter and the nurse sitting on the divan and the jacket hanging before the radiator; Elias Shomang was hidden by the door, but Steven in shirtsleeves crossed with a bottle of soda water, doing some imitation that made them all laugh.

Mrs Jarvis lost control of herself. Her hand left her coat and I saw an expanse of lace covering a vast flushed mound of flesh. "Yoo can't bring kaffirs in my bullding," she screamed. "Sitting there like this is a bloody backyard location, I mean to say, the other tenants is got a right to 'ev yoo thrown out. Kaffir women coming here, behaving like scum, living with decent people. Wha'd'yoo think, sitting here with kaffirs . . ."

Through the door, I saw that nobody in the room spoke, nobody looked at anybody else; the woman's voice took them like a seizure. It seemed to swell up and fill the flat, and I shouted back at her, my throat bursting, "This is my flat, d'you hear, you've no right to walk in here." But she went on and on: "Mr Hood! Mr Hood! Yoo got no right. I shoulda listened to what I been told. What would Mr McKay say, in his bullding, I got my job to think . . . place full of kaffirs. I know. I been told. Yoo coming home five o'clock in the morning in a kaffir taxi. Yoo unnerstend, Mr Hood . . ."

Steven said suddenly, standing in his shirtsleeves in the doorway between my room and the entrance, "You have no right, Toby. Look in your lease and you'll see." His voice was passionless and removed; I heard it like the voice of someone not present, a voice in one's brain. His brown, pale-palmed hands rested delicately on the door frame, he stood lightly, and his eyes were glitteringly bright.

The woman turned and went out the front door.

I still had my glass in my hand; I had never put it down — it had happened as quickly and unmomentously as that. Shomang was murmuring regret, like a guest who has broken an ashtray. The nurse sat staring down at her lap; she looked as if a hand must descend on her shoulder any minute. We were all a little incoherent, shaken, cocky. Peter, that sleepy boy, who lived like a snake in the charmer's basket, only coming to life with music, said, again and again, excitedly, "Bloody white bitches! Bloody white bitches!"

"Is it true about the lease?" I asked Steven.

"Of course. Haven't you got it?"

"Somewhere. I've never read it."

"Read it and see. No natives unless they're in the capacity of servants."

A World of Strangers, 1958

Rose lives in the backyard. She has lived there from the time when she washed the napkins of the children in the house, who are now university students. Her husband had disappeared before she took the job. Her lover, Ephraim, who works for Cerberus Security Guards, has lived with her in the yard for as long as anyone in the house can remember. He used to be night watchman at a parking garage, and the children, leaving for school in the morning after Rose had cooked breakfast for them, would meet "Rose's husband" in his khaki drill uniform, wheeling his bicycle through the gateway as he came off shift. His earlobes were loops that must once have been filled by ornamental plugs, his smile was sweetened by splayed front teeth about which, being what he was, who he was, he was quite unselfconscious.

That is what they remember, the day they hear that he is dead. The news comes by word-of-mouth, as all news seems to in the backyards of the suburb; who is in jail, caught without a pass, and must be bailed out, who has been told to leave a job and backyard at the end of the month, who has heard of the birth of a child, fathered on annual leave, away in the country.

"Blinder" from *Something Out There*, 1984

But it is over. Ephraim has been buried already; it's all over. She has heard about his death only after he has been buried because she is not the one to be informed officially. He has — had, always had — a wife and children there where he came from, where he was going back to, when he was killed. Oh yes. Rose knows about that. The lady of the house, the family, know about that; it was the usual thing, a young man comes to work in a city, he spends his whole life there away from his home because he has to earn money to send home, and so — the family in the house privately reasoned — his home really is the backyard where his town woman lives? As a socio-political concept the life is a paradigm (the grown child who is studying social science knows) of the break-up of families as a result of the migratory labour system. And that system (the one studying political science knows) ensures that blacks function as units of labour instead of living as men, with the right to bring their families to live in town with them.

"Blinder" from *Something Out There*, 1984

And they all came in to dinner. The chairs scraped in and out, the children changed places three times; they talked and laughed and no one had remembered to turn the radio down. The old man carved, the knife squeaking through juicy chicken flesh — and a potato shot off the dish and made a greasy patch on the tablecloth.

Elizabeth, you haven't given Master Peter a serviette.

Elizabeth, slice a lemon and bring it.

Elizabeth, another spoon.

The cheese that's wrapped in paper at the back of the refrigerator.

Bring some ice, please.

Elizabeth, why did you let the sauce go lumpy?

Bring a fresh tomato for Miss Vera.

When they had left the litter of the table Elizabeth put the drumstick and the pile of potatoes and the stump of cauliflower that was her dinner into the left-over warmth of the oven, to share later with her husband, and plunged to her elbows into the washing up. The old man went to lie down, the others sat about in the blue haze of the lounge, smoking and talking. And by the time Elizabeth had put away the dishes and cleaned the rim of grease and food from the sink, they were waiting for tea. Once again the kitchen added its voice to the voices, and the kettle hissed and frothed at the lid for attention while Elizabeth filled tarts with jam and buttered the scones.

And when tea was over they sat around amid the flagging talk and the forgotten cigarettes and realised that Sunday was almost gone again, ebbing with the heaviness in their stomachs and the red sun cut into red-hot bars by the railings of the balcony. Monday was coming. The freedom of Sunday wasn't freedom after all, but only a routine-dictated time of inactivity. They were waiting for Monday, that they hated; and that was the distaste, and the disappointment of it: Monday was better than Sunday.

No one remembered to call Elizabeth to clear away the tea-things. She stood in the passage a moment, her thick, set lips slightly open. Then swiftly and quietly, she closed the front door behind her so that it only clicked faintly, as a person clicks his tongue in a sleep, in response. The cold clear breath breathed out through the cement lungs of the city met her on the open corridor, seven layers above the tiny cement courtyard buried away below like the smallest of the Chinese boxes. Up she went, on the spiral back stair clinging like a steel creeper up the side of the building. And at the top, there was the roof, with something of the remoteness, the finality of all mountaintops. All around the sky was pink, streaky, and farther away than ever. A thin shadow of smoke aspiring like a kite from the chimney of the boiler room asserted this. The grey row of servant's rooms, one-eyed each with its small square window, looked down at the grey pebbles that covered the roof.

There was no one about. Bits of torn paper and empty lemonade bottles huddled against the balustrade. Elizabeth drew her foot out of her shoe and scratched the sole, hard and cracked with all her childhood of walking on hot bare earth, against her ankle. Beneath and around, as far as she could see, there was block after block of the city, nothing but spires and jutting rectangles of cement, deeply cleaved by black streets, and faintly smoking. Here and there, like a memory stirring, the fleck of a green tree.

"Monday Is Better Than Sunday"
from *The Soft Voice of the Serpent*, 1952

L ike a rope tied to one's ankle, the limits of their recognition in the ordinary life of the city constantly tripped one up in even the most casual attempt at a normal relationship with an African. Because I was white I continually forgot that Mary was not allowed here, could not use that entrance, must not sit on this bench. Like all urban Africans she had learned to walk warily between taboos as a child keeping on the squares and off the lines of paving.

The Lying Days, 1953

A senior farm worker with his wives, Thabazimbi, 1985.

House of the elder wife of the farm worker, Thabazimbi, 1985.

House of the younger wife of the farm worker, Thabazimbi, 1985.

77

Frederick Jillie, migrant worker, irons his dustcoat in the Jabulani Men's Hostel, Soweto. He sees his wife and children at his home in Queenstown, nearly 800 kilometers (500 miles) away, for two and a half weeks during his vacation each year. When the photograph was taken, in 1972, he had been living like this for thirteen years.

The bed of Velley Phakati, whose husband has gone away. The inscription on the pillow she embroidered reads, "Those who once met, will meet again." Soweto, 1972.

The servants' quarters of a city building, Jeppe Street, Johannesburg, 1984.

80

Woman crossing the street, Boksburg, 1979.

At evening, the low horizon of bush ran together as the light left it and seemed to sink over the edge of the world with the sun. And in the morning, it emerged again, a strangely even line of greyish trees, and, afar, was present all day. When we walked up to it, where it bordered the great mealie lands, it separated and thinned into growths of various characters; flat-topped, spreading trees with mean and sparse foliage; waist or shoulder-high bushes with short grass between them; low patches of briar; thickets of all three — trees, bush, and briar — through which not even the dog could crawl. And all these things were fanged with thorns. Everything that grew in this stunted forest had its particular weapon of thorn. The trees had long white spikes, clean and surgical-looking, like a doctor's instrument, giving off a powdery glitter in the sun. Some of the bushes had the same kind of thorn, but others had shorter, thicker ones, more like those of a rosebush, and some had thorns like fishhooks from which clothing, flesh, or fur could not easily be released. The aloes with their thick fleshy leaves were spiked with red thorns. But worst and cruellest were the black, shiny quills, so sharp and smooth that they slid into your skin as quickly as a hypodermic needle, that covered the trailing briars, ankle-high. As you tore through them you heard them clawing at your boots, and no matter how careful you tried to be, every now and then one would stab into your ankle or calf. If it did not break off in your flesh as you pulled free, it would tear a bloody groove through the skin, as if reluctant to let you go without a taste of your blood. If it broke off, it would fester in your flesh, just beyond the grasp of fingernails or tweezers, until the inflammation it had set up around itself softened and swelled the skin enough for you to press it out.

Walking through this landscape, so thinly green, so hostile with thorn that the living growth seemed a thing of steel rather than sap, I thought of old religious pictures, with their wildernesses and their bleeding, attenuated saints. This was a Gothic landscape, where the formalised pattern of interwoven thorns that often borders such pictures was real; where one could imagine a martyrdom symbolised by the brutality of these clutching, inanimate yet live instruments of malice.

In some places, where the bush had been cleared but the ground had not been ploughed for crops, fields of tall dead grass made a hissing noise as you pushed through it. Here and there, there was a break, and you would come upon a clearing where the low thorn briars spread over the earth, and no one, man or beast, could walk there. Bristling branches, which had no foliage to stir in the currents of the breeze and give them an air of life, maintained grim guard.

Grass like wood shavings, pinkish as if permanently touched with the light of sunset. Khaki weed, the growth of neglect and desolation, standing dead and high. The seed burs, round and sharp as porcupines, of some weed that had been cleared away, which crippled the dog the moment she set foot among them.

And more thorns — thorns in your hair and your hands, catching at your clothes, pulling you this way and that. And in silence. Silence on the fringes of which the soothing *sotto voce* of the doves, settling into the trees in some part of the bush which you never seemed to reach, was like the slowed heartbeat of the heat of the day. Now and then, the cheep, or the imagined cheep, of guinea fowl. Where, where, where?

A World of Strangers, 1958

The farm children play together when they are small; but once the white children go away to school they soon don't play together any more, even in the holidays. Although most of the black children get some sort of schooling, they drop every year farther behind the grades passed by the white children; the childish vocabulary, the child's exploration of the adventurous possibilities of dam, koppies, mealie lands and veld — there comes a time when the white children have surpassed these with the vocabulary of boarding-school and the possibilities of inter-school sports matches and the kind of adventures seen at the cinema. This usefully coincides with the age of twelve or thirteen; so that by the time early adolescence is reached, the black children are making, along with the bodily changes common to all, an easy transition to adult forms of address, beginning to call their old playmates *missus* and *baasie* — little master.

"Town and Country Lovers"
from *A Soldier's Embrace*, 1980

Tony was so happy helping to cook bricks in a serious mud-pie game with the farm labourers who called him "little master" (although that was Baasie's name) and playing with half-naked black children who were left behind when he and cousin Kobus ran into the farmhouse for milk and cake. I understood quite quickly that Baasie, with whom I lived in that house, couldn't have come here; I understood what Lily meant when she had said he wouldn't like to. I forgot Baasie. It was easy. No one here had a friend, brother, bed-mate, sharer of mother and father like him. Those who owed love and care to each other could be identified by a simple rule of family resemblance, from the elders enfeebled by vast flesh or wasting to the infant lying creased in the newly-married couple's pram. I saw it every Saturday, this human family defined by white skin. In the church to which my aunt drove us on Sunday morning, children clean and pretty, we sat among the white neighbours from farms round about and from the dorp, to whom the predikant said we must do as we would be done by. The waiter my uncle's barman beat with his lion's head belt was not there; he would be in his place down under the trees out of sight of the farmhouses, where black people sang hymns and beat old oildrums, or in the tin church in the dorp location. Harry Schutte didn't come to church (on Saturday nights roars of song and the sound of smashing glasses came from the bar, as farmers' rugby teams ended their afternoon's sport) but he had worked hard for his sleep-in and he never forgot an ice-cream for a kid who might have been one of his own (after all, he and my father were born in the same district). Daniel knew the strength of the tattooed arm he was safe from so long as he didn't take the white man's bottle but stayed content to swallow the dregs left in his glass.

For the man who had married my father's sister the farm "Vergenoegd" was God's bounty that was hers by inheritance, mortgage, land bank loan, and the fruitfulness he made of it, the hotel was his by the sign painted over the entrance naming him as licensee, the bottle store was his by the extension of that licence to off-sales. His sons would inherit by equally unquestioned right; the little boy who played with Tony would make flourish the tobacco, the pyrethrum — whatever the world thinks it needs and will pay for — Noel de Witt would never allow himself to grow.

When the girl cousin who was my contemporary was home from boarding-school for the weekend, we lady-shipped it about hotel and farm together as her natural assumption. Daniel was commanded to bring Cokes; the hotel cook was pestered to put dough men in the oven; a farm labourer mended her bicycle, a child from the kraal brought ants' eggs for her schoolfriend's grass snake, a kitchen maid had to wash and iron the particular dress she decided to wear. Her mother had no other claim, no other obligation but to please her daughter.

With this cousin I shared the second half of my name; it was the name of our common grandmother, long dead. Marie showed me our grandmother's grave, fenced in with several others of the family, on the farm. MARIE BURGER was cut into a mirror of smooth grey stone veined with glitter. On the slab were round glass domes cloudy with condensation under which plastic roses had faded.

You thought I must be named for Rosa Luxemburg, and the name I have always been known by as well as the disguised first half of my given name does seem to signify my parents' desire if not open intention. They never told me of it. My father often quoted that other Rosa; although he had no choice but to act the Leninist role of the dominant professional revolutionary, he believed that her faith in elemental mass movement was the ideal approach in a country where the mass of people were black and the revolutionary elite disproportionately white. But my double given name contained also the claim of MARIE BURGER and her descendants to that order of life, secure in the sanctions of family, church, law — and all these contained in the ultimate sanction of colour, that was maintained without question on the domain, dorp and farm, where she lay. *Peace. Land. Bread.* They had these for themselves.

Burger's Daughter, 1979

84

They are quite a delegation; the whole family expects to go along if there's an outing of any kind on a Sunday afternoon. Old De Beer has brought young De Beer, and young De Beer has with him young Mrs De Beer and child. There is also an adolescent girl who looks like young Mrs De Beer, probably a sister. He has seen them all, or a similar combination of the family, looking out from under ceremonious hats, when their car passed on their way home from church on the farm road, this morning. That's how they knew he'd be at the farm.

They are people who won't dispose themselves about a room until you tell them to. Come in, come in, sit down . . . They stand grouped slightly behind old De Beer. Please come inside.

Even when they are settled (looking round at the chair seats before placing their backsides, as if they're afraid of sitting on something or doing some damage) they remain hidden behind his shirt-tails — they don't speak. The child is so bashful, she's a vine wound to her mother's thick, young, knees-together legs. Hansie De Beer runs the farm, he's the one Mehring usually deals with but in his father's presence he ventures no opinions unless the old man turns his face to him. Old De Beer is a handsome man, his clothes filled drum-tight with his body; there ought to be a watch-chain across it, but there isn't, he wears on his wrist instead the latest Japanese electronic watch with a dial like something off an instrument panel. The retaining wall of belly and bunch of balls part the thighs majestically. Oh to wear your manhood, fatherhood like that, eh, stud and authority. The coatsleeves are stuffed with flesh that gives the arms the angle to lie monumentally on chair-arms — Mehring is going over these stock points, forgetting his duty to offer beer. The old man's Kaiser face, Edward VII face, regards him unyieldingly a moment; the son and the woman don't respond. Christ, they probably don't drink on Sundays, the son is afraid to say yes.

The old man's hoarse slow voice: —Perhaps if you've got brandy. I'll take a brandy.—

—Easy now, for Hansie. — Thanks very much, beer.

—Have you perhaps got a cold drink?— The wife makes a soft, little girl's request, she wouldn't be allowed to drink in front of the father-in-law anyway, Sunday or no Sunday.

The Conservationist, 1974

I've been to see the Nels. They were glad I came. I had always been welcome any time. There's a Holiday Inn where the commercial travellers mostly go, now. But the off-sales trade is unaffected. The Vroue Federasie has its annual meeting in a private room at the Holiday Inn, Auntie Velma told me (distracted for a moment from her trouble), even though it's licensed premises. And the chief of the nearby Homeland comes to lunch in the restaurant with the white mining consultants who are looking into the possibility that there's tin and chrome in his "country."

The Coen Nels are bewildered. I hadn't realized it could be such an overwhelming state of mind. More than anything else — bewildered. They were so proud of her, in a quasi-government position, speaking a foreign language; the brains of your side of the family, but put to the service of her country, boosting our agricultural produce. So proud of Marie, her sophisticated life — all this time imagining Paris as the Champs-Elysées pictured in the cheap prints sold to backveld hotels.

At the farm I asked to be put in one of the rondavels instead of the main house. They didn't argue on grounds of offended hospitality; when people are in trouble they somehow become more understanding of unexplained needs or whims, don't they. Walking at night after these dousing rains, the farm house, the sheds sheer away from me into a ground-mist you can lick off your lips. Wine still isn't served at the table but Uncle Coen made us drink brandy. I moved unevenly through drenched grass, I bumped into the water-tank, I thought only my legs were affected but I suppose my head was. I put my ear to the side of the stone barn wall where bees nest in the cavity, and heard them on the boil, in there. Layer upon layer of night concealed them. I walked round, not through, the shadows of walls and sheds, and on the bonnets of the parked cars light from somewhere peeled away sheets of dark and shone. Like fluttering eyelashes all about me: warmth, damp, and insects. I broke the stars in puddles. It's so easy to feel close to the soil, isn't it; no wonder all kinds of dubious popular claims are made on that base. The strong searchlights the neighbouring farmers have put up high above their homesteads, now, show through black trees. Headlights move on the new road; the farmlands are merging with the dorp. But it's too far away to hear a yell for help. If they came out now from behind the big old syringa trees with the nooses of wire left from kids' games in the branches, and the hanging length of angle iron that will be struck at six in the morning to signal the start of the day's work, if they loped out silently and put a Russian or Cuban machine-gun at my back, or maybe just took up (it's time?) a scythe or even a hoe —that would be it: a solution. Not bad. But it won't happen to me, don't worry. I went to bed in the rondavel and slept the way I had when I was a child, thick pink Waverley blankets kicked away, lumpy pillow punched under my neck. Anyone may have come in the door and looked down on me; I wouldn't have stirred.

Burger's Daughter, 1979

He's left the door open. She saw it; saw the gaping door, and the wind bellying the long curtains and sending papers skimming about the room, the leaves sailing in and slithering across the floors. The whole house was filing up with the wind. There had been burglaries in the suburb lately. This was one of the few houses without an alarm system — she and Arthur had refused to imprison themselves in the white man's fear of attack on himself and his possessions. Yet now the door was open like the door of a deserted house and she found herself believing, like any other suburban matron, that someone must enter. They would come in unheard, with that wind, and approach through the house, black men with their knives in their hands. She, who had never submitted to this sort of fear ever in her life, could hear them coming, hear them breathe under their dirty rag masks and their *tsotsi* caps. They had killed an old man on a farm outside Pretoria last week; someone described in the papers as a mother of two had held them off, at her bedside, with a golf club. Multiple wounds, the old man had received, multiple wounds.

She was empty, unable to summon anything but this stale fantasy, shared with the whole town, the whole white population. She lay there possessed by it, and she thought, she violently longed — they will come straight into the room and stick a knife in me. No time to cry out. Quick. Deep. Over.

The light came instead. Her sons began to play the noisy whispering games of children, about the house in the very early morning.

"The Life of the Imagination"
from *Selected Stories*, 1976

Landscape in the Waterberg, Transvaal, 1985.

The Nederduits Gereformeerde Kerk (Dutch Reformed Church), Lothair, Transvaal, 1984.

Farmer's son with his nursemaid, Marico Bushveld, 1964.

On an old Transvaal farm near Fochville: the farmer's wife, 1965.

92

Oom Flip du Toit on the stoep of his farm workshop, Marico Bushveld, 1964.

Farmer, Johannes van der Linde, with his head labourer, Ou Sam, near Bloemfontein, 1965.

Tsotsis with Okapi knife, Soweto, 1972.

She stood in the open bathroom doorway gazing at him across the passage into the living-room; her bare feet and shoulders were free of a big bath-towel. She said nothing, did not even whisper. The flat seemed to shake with the strong unhurried blows.

He made as if to go to the door, at last, but now she ran and clutched him by both arms. She shook her head wildly; her lips drew back but her teeth were clenched, she didn't speak. She pulled him into the bedroom, snatched some clothes from the clean laundry laid out on the bed and got into the wall-cupboard, thrusting the key at his hand. Although his arms and calves felt weakly cold he was horrified, distastefully embarrassed at the sight of her pressed back crouching there under his suits and coat; it was horrible and ridiculous. *Come out!* he whispered. *No! Come out!* she hissed: *Where? Where can I go?*

Never mind! Get out of there!

He put out his hand to grasp her. At bay, she said with all the force of her terrible whisper, baring the gap in her teeth: *I'll throw myself out the window.*

She forced the key into his hand like the handle of a knife. He closed the door on her face and drove the key home in the lock, then dropped it among coins in his trouser pocket.

He unslotted the chain that was looped across the flat door. He turned the serrated knob of the Yale lock. The three policemen, two in plain clothes, stood there without impatience although they had been banging on the door for several minutes. The big dark one with an elaborate moustache held out in a hand wearing a plaited gilt ring some sort of identity card.

Dr von Leinsdorf said quietly, the blood coming strangely back to legs and arms, "What is it?"

The sergeant told him they knew there was a coloured girl in the flat. They had had information; "I been watching this flat three months, I know."

"Town and Country Lovers"
from *A Soldier's Embrace*, 1980

The high-school boys and girls who clambered onto the train every morning on their way to school in the next Witwatersrand town (Noorddorp's high school couldn't accommodate them all, before the new high schools were built) didn't notice old Van As or his cough. They filled his carriage and a number of others, willy-nilly, yelling and fooling, great, well-grown South African children whose legs and bodies defeated the purpose of school uniform so thoroughly that, on them, it was not modest and drab but robustly provocative, in the best vaudeville tradition. The girls' short serge gym-frocks showed inches of thigh above black stockings straining to cover strong, curved legs and bulging calves; heavy breasts jutted under the tightly buttoned shirts. The enormous hairy legs of boys in football shorts that barely contained their muscular buttocks, stretched across the aisles; at fourteen or fifteen they weighed 170 pounds and had the terrifying belly-laugh that comes with newly-broken voices and new beards breaking erratically through adolescent pimples. They wrote four-letter words on the carriage doors. They stuck gum on the seats and pummelled and flirted, and were as unmindful of old Van As as they were of everyone else outside the violent and raucous orbit of their time of life.

"The Last Kiss"
from *Selected Stories*, 1976

He looked at Jennifer and her clothes, and thought of the way a white woman could look: one of those big, soft, European women with curly yellow hair, with very high-heeled shoes that made them shake softly when they walked, with a strong scent, like hot flowers, coming up, it seemed, from their jutting breasts under the lace and pink and blue and all the other pretty things they wore —women with nothing resistant about them except, buried in white, boneless fingers, those red, pointed nails that scratched faintly at your palms.

"Which New Era Would That Be"
from *Selected Stories*, 1976

Afterwards she sat on the veranda. She smoked and rested her eyes on the horizon of sea. The sun was behind the house in the afternoons and the shadow that fell before it was deep, the brightness beyond it searching. The curtains bellying convex then concave on the windows that gave onto the far end of the veranda remained closed. She thought of him, going over him slowly and repeatedly, as if she were describing him. A black man sitting in the car, with the small ears they have and the tiny whorls of felted black hair. ("Wool": but where was it like the soft, oily, or silky washed fleece of sheep?) A black man like the thousands, the kaffir and piccanin and native and nig of her childhood, the "African" of her adult life and friendships; the man; the lover. He was these. And none of them. Shibalo. When she saw his back, in the car, he was for a steady moment all the black men that had been around her through her life, familiar in the way of people not known as individuals. She had known him in this way a long, long time; the other way hardly at all, by comparison. Did he pick his nose as some of the other Africans she had been friendly with did, out of nervous habit, while he argued? These were things one got to know, as well as the quality of the mind, when one began to enter into individual relationships with people. Frenchmen and Germans cleaned their teeth with slivers of wood while you were eating. What did she do, when she was alone or in the other aloneness of intimacy, that offended against the ideal of a creature, living, but not decaying, that is kept up in public? Tom pared his toenails and let the cuttings from the clippers fly about the bedroom, so that she sometimes found a piece of sharp, yellowish rind in the bed or fallen into an open drawer. She felt some revulsion always but it passed because she was in love with him sexually; his flesh was alive for her: therefore he was dying continually. Perhaps you can accept the facts of renewal through decay only where there is love of the flesh.

She was waiting for the moment when the man appeared from the sleep and silence behind the curtains. She had the feeling, half mean, half powerful, of a person of whom something is going to be asked. What did he expect of her, Gideon Shibalo? You had always to do things for them because they were powerless to do anything for you. But did this mean that there was no limit to it, no private demarcation that anyone might be allowed to make before another? Because he has no life here among us, must I give him mine?—

Occasion for Loving, 1963

99

In respectful silences for the weakness of our sex, the flesh that can come upon any of us as women, black matrons were handed slowly, backside and belly, along past knees to the table where Flora had a microphone rigged up. Others spoke from where they sat or stood, suddenly set apart by the gift of tongues, while the faces wheeled to see. The old white woman's crusade turned out to be road safety, a campaign in which "our Bantu women must pull together with us" — she trembled on in the sweet, chuckly voice of a deaf upper-class English-woman while Flora tried to bring the discourse to an end with flourishing nods. A redhead whose expression was blurred by freckles floral as her dress asked passionately that the meeting launch a Courtesy Year to promote understanding between the races. She had her slogan ready, SMILE AND SAY THANKS. There was a soft splutter of tittering crossed by a groan of approval like some half-hearted response in church, but a young white woman jumped up with fists at her hips— Thank you for what? Maybe the lady has plenty to thank for. But was the object of action for women to make black women "thankful" for the hovels they lived in, the menial jobs their men did, the inferior education their children got? Thankful for the humiliation dealt out to them by white women living privileged, protected lives, who had the vote and made the laws—

Burger's Daughter, 1979

" " I don't know how you can say so. There isn't plenty of time at all. You know we had to fill in the registration form last year. They've got my name and everything. You know that when I went with the school tour I couldn't even get a passport to go overseas without you writing to Pretoria for permission from the Defence Force. As soon as the exams are over at the end of the year — this year — (underlined twice) they'll call me up. Please, dad, I know you're busy and that but I must know. Am I going to America in December or not. That's what I must know. (Crossed out.) All I can tell you, that if anyone thinks I am going into their army to learn to 'kill kaffirs' like a *ware ou*, well I'm damn well not. Thank you very much — you say it will be an experience for me to meet all sorts of people I don't normally, being sent to a good — I'd call it snob, by the way — school. What sort of people? I don't see anything good (crossed out) anything to be gained by living for nine months as a cropped head with a bunch of loyal South Africans learning how to be the master race because you've got the guns. It would be a good experience, too, I suppose, to be sent up to the Caprivi Strip to shoot Freedom Fighters."

The Conservationist, 1974

No wonder most of them talked in the end. It was hard enough to do a number of shifts with them during the day or night, with breaks in between for a cup of coffee, something to eat, and best of all, a walk outside in the street; whereas most of them, like this tough nut he was handling with the Major now, were questioned by a roster of personnel twenty-four, thirty-six hours non-stop. And, as the Major had taught, even when these people were given coffee, a cigarette, allowed to sit down, they knew they were being watched and had to watch themselves all the time, for what they might let slip. It was one of the elementary lessons of this work that the gratification of a draw of smoke into the lungs might suddenly succeed in breaking the stoniest will and breaching trained revolutionary hostility towards and contempt for interrogators. (The Major was a very clever, highly-educated and well-read man — you had to have someone like that for the class of detainee that was coming in these days, they'd just run rings round someone who'd only got his matric.) The Major said it didn't even matter if you got to feel sorry for them — the Major knew about this, although you always hid it; ''a bond of sympathy'' was the first real step on the way to extracting a confession. Well, Sergeant Chapman didn't have any such feelings today. Inside his uniform his body was filled with the sap of sun and fresh air; the sight of the sleepless, unshaven man standing there, dazed and smelly (they sweated even if they shivered, under interrogation) made him sick (the Major warned that occasional revulsion was natural, but unproductive).

Why couldn't these people live like any normal person? A man with this one's brains and university degrees, English-speaking and whatnot, could become a big shot in business instead of a trade unionist letting a bunch of blacks strike and get him in trouble. When you interrogated a detainee, you had to familiarize yourself with all the details supplied by informers for his file; this one had a well-off father, a doctor wife, twin babies, an affair with a pretty student (admittedly, he had met her through her research connected with unions) and his parents-in-law's cottage at one of the best places for fishing on the coast, for his holidays. What more does a white man want? With a black man, all right, he wants what he can't have, and that can make a man sit eating his heart out in jail half his life. But how good to walk, on Saturday, to the dam where you used to swim as a kid, to be greeted (these people who incite blacks against us should just have seen) by the farm boys at the kraal with laughter and pleasure at your acquisition of a wife; to go out with your father to shoot jackals at sunset. There's something wrong with all these people who become enemies of their own country: this private theory was really the only aspect of his work — for security reasons — he talked about to his girl, who, of course (he sometimes smiled to forget), was now his wife. Something wrong with them. They're enemies because they can't enjoy their lives the way a normal white person in South Africa does.

''Something Out There''
from *Something Out There*, 1984

Witbooi offered to make a coffin. They used a tarpaulin in the meantime, weighted with stones from that place where the whites once cooked meat. Izak helped saw the planks at the work-shop near the house; Alina brought tea and porridge and stayed to talk, but not loudly, because of what it was the two men were hammering together. Jacobus had phoned the farmer in town at his office and asked for money for the wood. It was granted without questioning or difficulty, yes, all right, get it from the Indian and tell him he'll be paid. Jacobus knew, through Alina's daughter's husband (Christmas Club) that the India had wood stored from some building he had been doing. But the farmer didn't want to hear about it. He was leaving that day for one of those countries white people go to, the whole world is theirs. He gave some instructions over the phone; Jacobus must look after everything nicely.

Jacobus and Alina and one of the other women went to the Indian store together, with the pick-up, to fetch the wood. The women cried and said there was no money for a wrapping-cloth and wouldn't the India give them some material, anything, any piece of old cloth? He felt sorry for the poor devils, human after all, who must have lost a member of their family, and got one of his sons to cut a length from a roll of Japanese cotton that wasn't a good seller. They said God would bless him.

The funeral took place on high firm ground on a fine Thursday afternoon. Solomon and his brother had dug the grave. The coffin that now held properly what it should was put on the hay wagon hitched to the tractor and driven by Jacobus slowly enough for all to follow on foot. Plovers flew up peeping, shrilling, darting and diving ahead, raising their usual excitable alarm in a serenity of sky and land that took no note of them. The tractor rolled on. At the appointed spot, those people who had not followed were gathered; old Thomas the night-watchman did not sleep that afternoon, and the children stood by. The women and old men from the location who weeded the lands were there. So was Phineas's wife, but her followers were not with her. Thursday is the day when the women members of the sect of Zion meet in groups on the veld round about the location, and one of these appeared, led by a man in a long white coat with blue sashes criss-crossing it, carrying a tasselled staff, and accompanied by a man with a drum. He struck the drum softly once or twice: the sound of a sigh in space, the great sun-lit afternoon that surrounded the gathering. There was a moment of absolute silence when everyone was still, perhaps there was no need of speech, no one knew what to say, and then the one with the staff began to declaim and harangue, sometimes lifting a foot in the air as if to climb some invisible step, waving his staff. The women of his group, round white hats starched and ironed into the shape of four-petalled flower-bells, sang a hymn. He prayed aloud again and once more they sang, and Thomas's voice joined them in thin but perfect harmony. The eyes of the children moved with the spade. Phineas's wife's face was at peace, there was no burden of spirits on her shoulders as she watched Witbooi, Izak, Solomon, and Jacobus sink the decent wooden box, and her husband shovel the heavy spatter of soil, soft and thick. Without consulting Jacobus, Witbooi had privately provided a pile of medium-sized stones to surround the mound as he would mark out a flower-bed in a white man's garden.

The one whom the farm received had no name. He had no family but their women wept a little for him. There was no child of his present but their children were there to live after him. They had put him away to rest, at last; he had come back. He took possession of this earth, theirs; one of them.

The Conservationist, 1974

There are possibilities for me, certainly;
but under what stone do they lie?

— FRANZ KAFKA

Max's bomb, described in court as being made of a tin filled with a mixture of sulphur, saltpetre, and charcoal, was found before it exploded and he was arrested within twenty-four hours. Others were more or less successful and it all began again, and worse than it had ever been before; raids, arrests, detention without trial. The white people who were kind to their pets and servants were shocked at bombs and bloodshed, just as they had been shocked, in 1960, when the police fired on the men, women, and children outside the Sharpeville pass office. They can't stand the sight of blood; and again gave, to those who have no vote, the humane advice that the decent way to bring about change is by constitutional means. The liberal-minded whites whose protests, petitions, and outspokenness have achieved nothing remarked the inefficiency of the terrorists and the wasteful senselessness of their attempts. You cannot hope to unseat the great alabaster backside with a tinpot bomb. Why risk your life? *The madness of the brave is the wisdom of life.* I didn't understand, till then. Madness, God, yes, it was; but why should the brave ones among us be forced to be mad?

The Late Bourgeois World, 1966

Man sleeping, Joubert Park, Johannesburg, 1975.

Woman on a bench, Joubert Park, Johannesburg, 1975.

Miss Lovely Legs Competition at the Pick 'n' Pay Hypermarket, Boksburg, 1980.

Schoolboy with scrolls of merit, Boksburg, 1979.

Methodists meet to find ways of reducing the racial, cultural and class barriers which divide them, Daveytown, Benoni, 1980.

Funeral with military honours for two National Service men, boyhood friends, killed in the same action against SWAPO forces, on the Namibia-Angola border, Boksburg, 1980.

Funeral of trade union leader, Andries Raditsela, who died of
"unknown causes" shortly after release from detention in the hands of the Security Police,
Tsakane, Brakpan, 1985.

Combined police and army patrol in Duduza black township, Nigel, during the State of Emergency, 1985.
The policemen carry heavy whips known as sjamboks.

A child gives the salute of the banned African National Congress at the graves of four assassinated black community leaders, Cradock, Eastern Cape, 1985.

Fifteen year old youth after release from detention. 1985.

No one can defect.
I don't know the ideology:
It's about suffering.
How to end suffering.
And it ends in suffering. Yes, it's strange to live in a
country where there are still heroes.

Burger's Daughter, 1979

A NOTE ON THE TYPE

This book was set in a modern adaptation of a type designed by the first William Caslon (1692–1766), greatest of English letter founders. The Caslon face, an artistic, easily read type, has enjoyed two centuries of ever-increasing popularity in our own country. It is of interest to note that the first copies of the Declaration of Independence and the first paper currency distributed to the citizens of the newborn nation were printed in this typeface.

This book was composed by Micrographix, Newport, Rhode Island.
Films for 300-line screen duotone illustrations were prepared by Richard Benson.
The book was printed and bound by Universitätsdruckerei H. Stürtz AG,
Würzburg, Germany. The typography, layout, jacket, and binding design are by
Thomas Palmer.